Friends do not live in harmony merely, as some say, but in melody.

HENRY DAVID THOREAU (1817-1862)
American writer

Canadian representatives: General Publishing Co., Ltd., 30 Lesmill Road, Don Mills, Ontario M3B 2T6. International representatives: Worldwide Media Services, Inc., 30 Montgomery Street, Jersey City, New Jersey 07302. ISBN: 0-89471-162-8 paperback. This book may be ordered directly from the publisher. Please add $2.50 for postage. *But try your bookstore first!* Running Press Book Publishers, 125 South Twenty-second Street, Philadelphia, Pennsylvania 19103. Illustration by Amira Dvorah. Cover by Michael Green. Editor: Amy Shapiro.

The Friendship Notebook

A personal journal

Some of my best friends are children. In fact, all of my best friends are children.

J.D. SALINGER, b. 1919
American writer

Grief can take care of itself, but to get the full value of a joy you must have somebody to divide it with.

MARK TWAIN (1835-1910)
American writer

There are three types of friends: those like food, without which you can't live; those like medicine, which you need occasionally; and those like an illness, which you never want.

SOLOMON IBN GABIROL (1021-1058)
Hebrew poet, aphorist

Every time a friend succeeds I die a little.

GORE VIDAL, b. 1925
American writer

If you have one true friend
you have more than your share.

THOMAS FULLER (1654-1734)
English physician, writer

A friend is one who dislikes
the same people you dislike.

ANONYMOUS

It is said that love is blind. Friendship, on the other hand, is clairvoyant.

PHILIPPE SOUPAULT, (1897-1990)
French writer

Platonic love is love from the neck up.

THYRA SAMTER WINSLOW (1903-1961)
American drama and literary critic

"Yes'm, old friends is always best, 'less you can catch a new one that's fit to make an old one out of."

SARAH ORNE JEWETT (1849-1909)
American writer

I want everyone else I meet in the whole world
to like me, except the people I've already met,
handled, found inconsequential, and forgot about.

JOSEPH HELLER, b. 1923
American writer

Sooner or later you've heard about all your best friends have to say. Then comes the tolerance of real love.

NED ROREM, b. 1923
American journalist

Having someone wonder where you are when you don't come home at night is a very old human need.

MARGARET MEAD (1901-1978)
American anthropologist

My true friends have always given me that supreme proof of
devotion, a spontaneous aversion for the man I loved.

COLETTE (1873-1954)
French writer

Diamonds are a girl's best friend.

LEO ROBIN (1900–1984)
American songwriter

Here at the frontier, there are falling leaves.
Although my neighbors are all barbarians,
And you, you are a thousand miles away,
There are always two cups on my table.

T'ANG DYNASTY (618-906 A.D.)

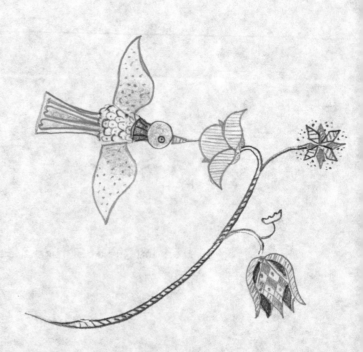

Men kick friendship around like a football, but it doesn't seem to crack. Women treat it like glass and it goes to pieces.

ANNE MORROW LINDBERGH, b. 1906
American writer, poet, aviator

After an acquaintance of ten minutes many women will exchange confidences that a man would not reveal to a lifelong friend.

PAGE SMITH, b. 1917
American historian

If we all told what we know of one another there would not be four friends in the world.

BLAISE PASCAL (1623-1662)
French philosopher

How I like to be liked,
and what I do to be liked!

CHARLES LAMB (1775-1834)
English writer

We tiptoed around each other
like heartbreaking new friends.

JACK KEROUAC (1922-1969)
American writer

Tell me who admires and loves you,
and I will tell you who you are.

CHARLES AUGUSTIN SAINTE-BEUVE (1804-1869)
French critic

I want someone to laugh with me, someone to be grave with me, someone to please me and help my discrimination with his or her own remark, and at times, no doubt, to admire my acuteness and penetration.

ROBERT BURNS (1759-1796)
Scottish poet

I do not want people to be very agreeable, as it saves me the trouble of liking them a great deal.

JANE AUSTEN (1775-1817)
English writer

My friends, there are no friends.

COCO CHANEL (1883-1971)
French fashion designer

Friendship is far more tragic than love.
It lasts longer.

OSCAR WILDE (1854-1900)
English writer

He who is the friend of all humanity
is not my friend.

MOLIERE (1622-1673)
French playwright

Oh dear! how unfortunate I am not to have anyone to weep with!

MADAME DE SEVIGNE (1626-1696)
French writer

Madam, I have been looking for a person who disliked gravy all my
life; let us swear eternal friendship.

SYDNEY SMITH (1771-1845)
English clergyman

My darling, be a wife, be a friend,
write good letters, do not mope,
do not torment me.

ANTON CHEKOV (1860-1904)
Russian writer

I want a sofa, as I want a friend,
upon which I can repose familiarly.

WILLIAM MAKEPEACE THACKERAY (1811-1863)
English writer

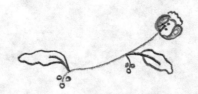

Each had his past shut in him like the leaves of a book known to him by heart; and his friends could only read the title.

VIRGINIA WOOLF (1882-1941)
English writer

Most people enjoy the inferiority of their friends.

LORD CHESTERFIELD (1694-1773)

. . .when people have light in themselves, it will shine out from them. Then we get to know each other as we walk together in the darkness, without needing to pass our hands over each other's faces, or to intrude into each other's hearts.

ALBERT SCHWEITZER (1875-1965)
German scholar, humanitarian

These can never be true friends: hope, dice, a prostitute, a robber, a cheat, a goldsmith, a monkey, a doctor, a distiller.

HINDU PROVERB

Perhaps only people who are capable of real
togetherness have that look of being alone in the
universe. . . the others have a certain stickiness.

D.H. LAWRENCE (1885-1930)
English writer

Friendship is almost always the union of a part of one mind with a part of another; people are friends in spots.

GEORGE SANTAYANA (1863-1952)
American writer

I step over to his table and give him a medium hello, and he looks up and gives me a medium hello right back, for, to tell you the truth, Maury and I are never bosom friends.

DAMON RUNYON (1880-1946)
American writer

Treat your friends as you do your pictures,
and place them in their best light.

JENNIE JEROME CHURCHILL (1854-1921)
English writer (mother of Winston Churchill)

Animals are such agreeable friends—they ask no questions, they pass no criticisms.

GEORGE ELIOT (1819-1880)
English writer

When a person that one loves is in the world and alive and well . . . then to miss them is only a new flavor, a salt sharpness in experience.

WINIFRED HOLTBY (1898-1935)
English writer

One passes through the world knowing few, if any, of the important things about even the people with whom one has been. . . in the closest intimacy.

ANTHONY POWELL, b. 1905
English writer

One friend in a lifetime is much; two are many; three are hardly possible.

HENRY ADAMS (1838-1918)
American writer

A friend knows how to allow for mere quantity in your talk, and only replies to the quality. . .

WILLIAM DEAN HOWELLS (1837-1920)
American writer

. . .to find a friend one must close one eye:
to keep him, two.

NORMAN DOUGLAS (1868-1952)
English novelist, scientist

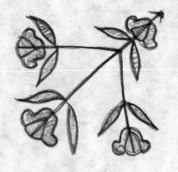

There are three faithful friends — an old wife,
an old dog, and ready money.

BENJAMIN FRANKLIN (1706-1790)
American diplomat, inventor

Every murderer is probably somebody's old friend.

AGATHA CHRISTIE (1890-1976)
English writer

Think twice before you speak to a friend in need.

AMBROSE BIERCE (1842-1914)
American writer

Devote six years to your work but in the seventh go into solitude
or among strangers, so that your friends, by remembering what
you were, do not prevent you from being what you have become.

LEO SZILARD (1898-1964)
Hungarian/Amercian nuclear physicist

Friendship is like money,
easier made than kept.

SAMUEL BUTLER (1835-1902)
English novelist, essayist

Unfortunately, in a long life one gets barnacled over
with the mere shells of friendship and it is difficult
without hurting oneself to scrape them off.

BERNARD BERENSON (1865-1959)
Polish/American art critic

Instead of loving your enemies,
treat your friends a little better.

EDGAR WATSON HOWE (1853-1937)
American writer

Constant use had not worn ragged
the fabric of their friendship.

DOROTHY PARKER (1893-1967)
American writer

Love and friendship are profoundly personal, selfish values . . . an expression and assertion of self-esteem, a response to one's own values in the person of another.

AYN RAND (1905–1982)
Russian/American writer

"Unbosom yourself," said Wimsey. "Trouble shared is trouble halved."

DOROTHY SAYERS (1893-1957)
English writer

All the world is queer save thee and me.
And even thou art a little queer.

ROBERT OWEN (1771-1858)
Welsh/American social reformer

What I cannot love, I overlook.
Is that real friendship?

ANAIS NIN (1903-1977)
French/American writer

Histories are more full of examples of the fidelity of dogs than of friends.

ALEXANDER POPE (1688-1744)
English poet

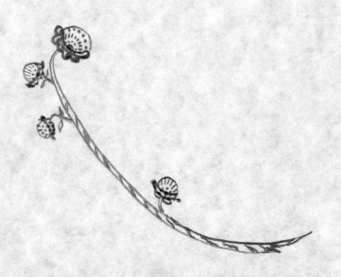

Only choose in marriage a woman whom you would choose as a friend if she were a man.

JOSEPH JOUBERT (1754-1824)
French philosopher

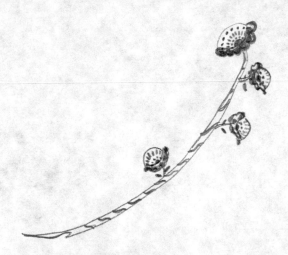

To want friendship is a great fault. Friendship ought to be a gratuitous joy, like the joys afforded by art, or life. . .

SIMONE WEIL (1909-1943)
French philosopher

Money can't buy friends, but you can get a better class of enemy.

SPIKE MILLIGAN, b. 1918
English comedian, writer

I no more like people personally than I like dogs. When I meet them I am only apprehensive whether they will bite me, which is reasonable and sensible.

STANLEY SPENCER (1891-1959)
English artist

We need two kinds of acquaintances, one to complain to, while we boast to the others.

LOGAN PEARSALL SMITH (1865-1946)
American/English writer

It is in the thirties that we want friends. In the forties we know they won't save us any more than love did.

F. SCOTT FITZGERALD (1896-1940)
American writer

. . .ours, that tea bag of a word which steeps in the conditional.

ELIZABETH HARDWICK, b. 1916
American writer, educator

Choose an author as you choose a friend.

WENTWORTH DILLON, Earl of Roscommon (1633-1685)
English nobleman

. . .because I got you to look after me, and you got me to look after you. . . We got each other, that's what, that gives a hoot in hell about us. . .

JOHN STEINBECK (1902-1968)
American writer

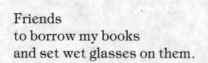

Friends
to borrow my books
and set wet glasses on them.

EDWIN ARLINGTON ROBINSON (1869-1935)
American poet

If you want a person's faults, go to
those who love him. They will not tell you,
but they know.

ROBERT LOUIS STEVENSON (1850-1894)
American writer

And the song, from beginning to end,
I found in the heart of a friend.

HENRY WADSWORTH LONGFELLOW (1807-1882)
American poet

There was nothing remote or mysterious here — only something private. The only secret was the ancient communication between two people.

EUDORA WELTY, b. 1909
American writer

If I had to choose between betraying my country and betraying my friend, I hope I should have the guts to betray my country.

E.M. FORSTER (1879-1970)
English writer

. . .they grew to be so happy that even when they were two worn-out old people they kept on. . .playing together like dogs.

GABRIEL GARCIA MARQUEZ, b. 1928
Colombian writer

A companion loves some agreeable qualities which a man may possess, but a friend loves the man himself.

JAMES BOSWELL (1740-1795)
Scottish biographer, lawyer

The differences between friends cannot but reinforce their friendship.

MAO TSE-TUNG (1893-1976)
Chinese leader

A woman wants her friends to be perfect. She sets a pattern . . .
lays a friend out on this pattern and worries and prods at any little
qualities which do not coincide with her own image.

BETTY MACDONALD (1908-1958)
American writer

The richer your friends, the more they will cost you.

ELISABETH MARBURY (1856-1933)
American theatrical agent

. . . being with you is like walking on a very clear
morning — definitely the sensation of belonging there.

E.B. WHITE (1899-1985)
American writer

When you are down and out, something always turns up — and it is usually the noses of your friends.

ORSON WELLES (1915-1985)
American actor, director

Friendship is unnecessary, like philosophy, like art. . . It has no survival value; rather it is one of those things that give value to survival.

C.S. LEWIS (1898-1963)
English writer

I no doubt deserved my enemies, but I don't believe I deserved my friends.

WALT WHITMAN (1819-1892)
American poet

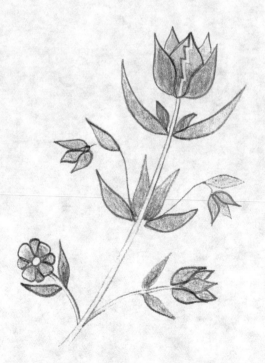

Friends are a second existence.

BALTASAR GRACIAN (1601-1658)
Spanish satirist, writer

The only thing to do is to hug one's friends tight and do one's job.

EDITH WHARTON (1862-1937)
American writer

If two people who love each other let a single instant wedge itself between them, it grows — it becomes a month, a year, a century; it becomes too late.

JEAN GIRAUDOUX (1882-1944)
French playwright

It is good to have some friends
both in Heaven and in Hell.

GEORGE HERBERT (1593-1633)
English writer

Friendship is a very taxing and arduous form
of leisure activity.

MORTIMER ADLER, b. 1902
American educator

I never met a man I didn't like.

WILL ROGERS (1879-1935)
American humorist

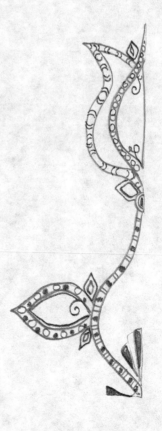

Each friend represents a world in us, a world possibly not born until they arrive, and it is only by this meeting that a new world is born.

ANAIS NIN (1903-1977)
French/American writer

What is important to a relationship is a harmony of emotional roles and not too great a disparity in the general level of intelligence.

MIRRA KOMAROVSKY, b. 1906
Russian/American educator

Friendship or love — one must choose.
One cannot serve two masters.

RENÉ CREVEL (1900-1935)
French writer

Wherever you are it is your own friends
who make your world.

WILLIAM JAMES (1842-1910)
American psychiatrist

Louis, I think this is the beginning
of a beautiful friendship.

RICK BLAINE
Saloon owner (in the film "Casablanca")